Passing on the Left

Stories of Gifted Individuals

Passing on the Left

Stories of Gifted Individuals

Patricia Farrenkopf, Ed.D

Owner and Creator of

PGi TM

ProGift-ify

Fishtail Publishing

Passing on the Left

Book design by Erin O'Neil
www.erinoneil.org

Cover design by Erin O'Neil

Fishtail Publishing

Published in the USA by Fishtail Publishing LLC
Westerville, OH

www.fishtailpublishing.org

ISBN: 978-1-7333380-6-6
Library of Congress Control Number: 2021900291

This book is dedicated to all of the gifted individuals I have had the pleasure of knowing and working with who have had a need to pass on the left. It is my hope that you passed on the left successfully and safely. Thank you for sharing your lives with me.

Table of Contents

Every time I see an adult on a bicycle,
I no longer despair for the future of the human race.

H.G. Wells, writer (Sep 21, 1866-1946)

Introduction

My husband and I live just right around the corner from the Ohio to Erie Trail. The one way distance from Cleveland to Cincinnati is 326 miles. It is one of several available trails in the state of Ohio created by a vision from the Ohio Department of Natural Resources: Division of Parks and Watercraft and our state legislature. Public input and a trail inventory led to partnerships, collaboration, funding, marketing, and promotion of the multi-use, natural surface, motorized, mountain bike, equestrian, and water trails (Arbour, 2019).

We used to ride our bicycles on the Westerville portion of the trail and run 5 miles to uptown Westerville and back. Now, we mostly enjoy the path for walking, either on a morning jaunt or on a trip to the local grocery store. We often see neighbors and friends using the path, but also have made new acquaintances coming from near or far. Some are biking, others are running, some rollerblading and others skateboarding. Babies in tagalongs and seniors from the independent living residence equate into usage by those from near birth to 100 years. Some ride from Cleveland to Cincinnati and then return. Others use just a section of the trail, many on a daily basis. It is possible for anyone who wants to make the trip to do so. Still, others elect to get from Cleveland to Cincinnati in a car.

As a courtesy and best practice, those using the path who can go faster than others in front of them will audibly say, "Passing on the left." After all, we are sharing the path with those using many different modes of transportation with different ability and agility levels. That does not make one user on the path better than another, but simply means that the right thing to do is create an environment where everyone can go at their own pace. Some adults ride alone or in groups, some children ride alone or with other children or their parents. All learn to say, "Passing on the left" when the need arises. Parents model that for their children and can provide the verbal signaling themselves.

In all 50 states, people on bikes are required to follow the same rules as drivers of other vehicles. Sounds good, right? Not so fast. Let's start with Title 45 of the Ohio Revised Code. Title 45 contains the laws that govern operation of all vehicles on Ohio roads, including bicycles. The laws describe what a driver is required to do or prohibited from doing. But laws do not tell people how to drive. That is the function of a driver's manual.

All Ohio laws are in the Ohio Revised Code and the Traffic Laws in Title 45. If you go to the library and want to find these laws on the shelf, the entire Ohio Revised Code is easy to find – they are bright red. The traffic laws found in Chapter 4511 of Title 45 contains the "Rules of the Road".

These are only the state laws. Ohio is known as a "Home Rule" state. The "Home Rule" provision in the Ohio Constitution allows local governments to pass their own laws. There are 88 counties in Ohio and hundreds of cities, villages, and other political, "ordinance-passing" entities. Each political body can and does pass its own laws. You will find local laws governing bicycle riding in many of these municipalities. Some of these local laws are nonsensical and contrary to state law, not to mention contrary to common sense.

You Might Be Asking Yourself, "What Does THIS Have to Do with Gifted Individuals?"

First, let's look at federal and state law for exceptional education populations. Public Law 94-142, the Education for All Handicapped Children Act, was enacted by Congress in 1975. This law, amended in 1997, is currently known as the Individuals with Disabilities Education Act (IDEA). The purpose of this law was to assure rights for our handicapped students, to meet their individual needs, and to improve the level of achievement for these identified students. For 45 years, this legislation has provided a national and state focus on providing appropriate services for this population. Early identification and services for preschool age children and public school special education students has provided the least restrictive environment for education in each student's neighborhoods and schools. Even during the global pandemic of 2020, continuing to provide special education identification and services has been a priority (IDEA News and Updates 2020). Funding for special education is provided through the IDEA Part B funding support provision of special education services to children with disabilities who are ages 3 to 21 in Ohio.

Now, let's look at gifted services at the federal and state levels. There is, unfortunately, no consistent federal law for identifying and serving gifted children and adolescents. At our state level, we have Gifted Operating Standards which mandate how students are identified and the need to notify parents and guardians. There is no mandate to serve, but if a district decides to count children as gifted and served, they must have a written education plan for their education. What is happening for our gifted students during the global pandemic? Even less structure and more inconsistencies (National Association for Gifted

Children, 2020). Funding for gifted education in Ohio is from individual school districts who report how much they spend each year on their designed services – if they have any.

Passing on the Left for Gifted Individuals

Many gifted students and their parents/guardians do not have knowledge of the existing paths or the way to get there. Once they find a way to the path, they need to find the best path (enrichment or acceleration) and the best vehicle to use as they progress (selecting from a continuum of services). As advocates, we need to teach them to advocate for themselves and be involved in the decision to Pass on the Left. Passing on the left can mean this path and vehicle as described in the Gifted Operating Standards (2018. pp. 5, 6):

Instruction that is differentiated from the standard curriculum for that course in depth, breadth, complexity, pace, and/or where content is above-grade level and occurring during the typical instructional day with flexibility allowed for the scheduling of district-approved internships or mentorships and higher education coursework, including credit flexibility.

Instructional time, class size, and caseload ratios for all service settings equivalent to districtwide instructional time, class size, and caseload ratios for the corresponding subject, grade level, and setting.

A continuum of services provided by each district board of education, where content is delivered, including but is not limited to such options as the following:

1. *A full-time self-contained classroom where the gifted intervention specialist is the teacher of record and all students are identified as gifted. A maximum of twenty students at one time is permitted in this setting.*

2. *A single subject self-contained course where the gifted intervention specialist is the teacher of record and all students are identified as gifted.*

3. *Services through co-teaching in a cluster grouping setting where a group of students who are gifted is deliberately placed together in a classroom where one teacher is a gifted intervention specialist with a maximum of twenty students who are gifted at any one time and a maximum caseload of eighty students who are gifted. The teachers shall be provided with regularly scheduled collaborative planning time. Each student served in this setting shall be provided instruction for no less than one core content class period a day or an average of fifteen percent of the school week.*

4. *A resource room/pull-out where the gifted intervention specialist has a maximum of twenty students who are gifted at any one time and a maximum caseload of eighty students who are gifted. Each student served in this setting shall be provided instruction for no less than one core content class period a day or an average of fifteen percent of the school week.*

5. *Cluster grouping where a small group of students who are gifted is deliberately placed together in a classroom. Each student served in this setting shall be provided instruction for no less than one core content class period a day or an average of fifteen percent of the school week.*

6. *An honors course*

7. *An international baccalaureate course*

8. *An advanced placement course*

9. *Services through a trained arts instructor*

10. *Grade acceleration, early entrance to kindergarten or first grade, subject acceleration, or early graduation from high school per district acceleration*

11. *Dual enrollment opportunities, including but not limited to college credit plus*

12. *Internships and mentorships*

13. *Educational options including credit flexibility, advanced online courses and programs*

14. *Services for students shall be consistent with their area(s) of identification and shall be*

15. *Differentiated to meet their needs.*

Just as with the paths and vehicles in Ohio envisioned by ODNR, there are choices depending upon your identification per each school district's policy and procedure for Gifted Services. Also, just as with Ohio vehicle laws, the availability of services can be different depending upon the school district in which you reside. Not all decision makers know about the overexcitabilities of gifted, nor do all understand the myths and realities of being gifted. Also, not all understand the non-linear development of identity or think about how systems (like the school district) can impact that journey. Advocates and gifted individuals, often one and the same, need to understand these qualities in order to weave through the maze that is being gifted.

What follows are stories of gifted individuals* who are more different from each other than they are alike. Overexcitabilities, myths, and their identity journey provide a unique tapestry – their own Passing on the Left story. See if you can fill in this chart as you experience their scenarios. As you read their stories, do any of them sound like you?

**Real names have been replaced by pseudonyms.*

Passing on the Left	Sensational Sensibilities	Myth or Reality	Identity Journey
	Awarenesses – Sensual Energetic – Psychomotor Feelings – Emotions Imagining – Imagination Thinking – Intellectual	Myths that are believed by the gifted individual or others in the family, friends,and/or larger community	Frames Recognition - Validation Confirmation - Affirmation Connections - Affiliation Preferences – Affinity Compass Contributors You Your Immediate Family Your Ancestry Your Origins Career Explorations Living Spaces Educational Routes Relationships Experiences Legislations Attributes Phases
Merry			
Merry's mom			
Gavin			
The Essexers			
Jonathan			

The meaning of life is to find your gift.
The purpose of life is to give it away.

Pablo Picasso

The Story of Merry - and also Merry's mom

This is Merry.

This is Merry's mom

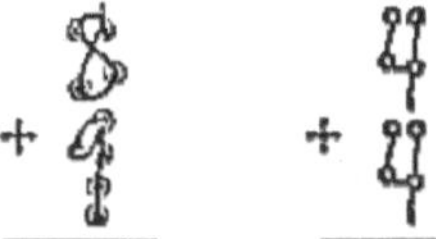

It was the beginning of November during Merry's first grade school year. Merry's mom explained to me the beginning of her daughter's challenges:

Merry has a weekly test on single-digit addition for the sake of fact fluency.

One Friday, upon coming home from school, Merry presented her take home folder. She went to her bedroom to change into her play clothes. When she came back into the kitchen, Merry asked her mom, "Did you clean out my folder yet?"

Mom replied to Merry, "Not yet," in her usual melodic voice.

Merry responded, "I made you a picture today. See? Here!"

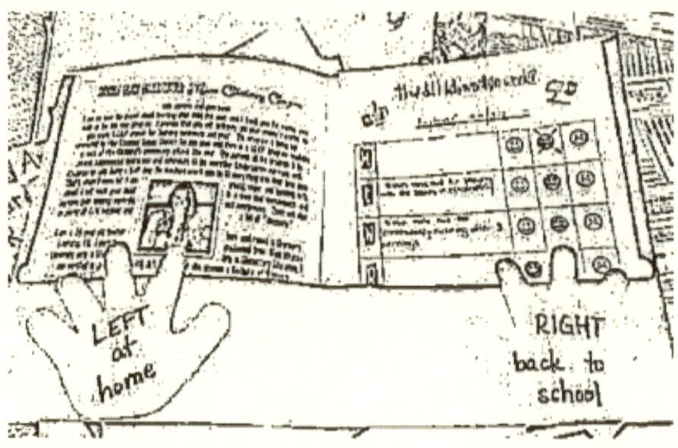

Note the folder organization: left is left at home and right goes right back to school.

The picture Merry created for her mom.

Merry's mom commented on her picture, "That is beautiful!" Then, Merry's mom noticed that there was something on the other side. It was the weekly test on single-digit addition for the sake of fact fluency.

Merry's mom said, "There's a math test on the back. You got an eight out of ten. Was it hard for you?"

Merry responded casually, "No. I only did eight out of ten."

Merry's mom continued her questioning, "Did you run out of time?"

Merry patiently explained to her mom, "No, I am the fastest one in the class."

Merry further pointed out, "It is still an 80 percent. That is a B." Merry's mom pressed on, "Yes, but you usually get a 100."

So, Merry finally summed it all up in a very calm and confident fashion, "Yes, but I got bored. We take that same test every week. I knew the first 8 were right, and they are worth ten points each, so that's an 80. I used the extra time to make you a picture."

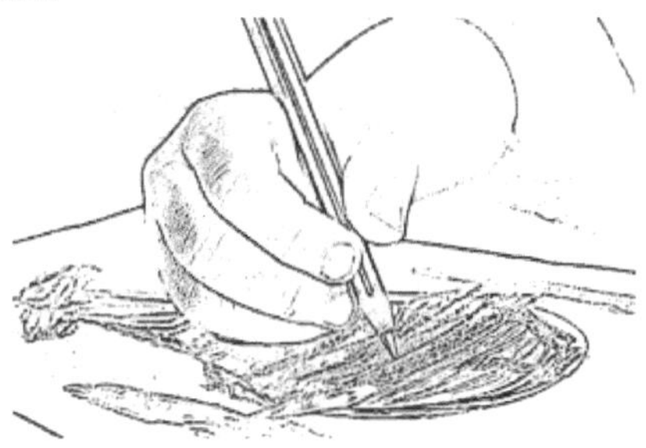

Merry's mom responded at first by saying the only thing she could think of in the moment...

Merry continued by sharing her inspiration for creating the picture. "See," she said, flipping the test over to the other side. "That's Jane Goodall and her mother at their Gombe camp in Tanzania, just like we are going to do someday, only we are going to live in the Amazon."

Looking at her mom, Merry observed, "You don't look happy."

Merry's mom processed the explanation and then gave some motherly words of advice, "The picture is a very good picture. You are very sweet and I would love to go to the Amazon with you because I love you and because I really wanted to be a zoologist. However, I would like for you to answer all of the questions on your test from now on."

Then, Merry came in with the match, point, set, "Okay. But don't worry about this time. We only get checks and minuses on our report card, and that is a check. Can we hang my picture on the fridge?"

While reflecting with me on this incident, Merry's mom shared more of her thoughts, "I am very careful about what I share with others in her school, because even just the label of 'gifted' leaves a mark. We are dealing with the expectation that, if she is really gifted, she should be a model student. In reality, she is all but falling out of her desk, doing 80% of her work, writing field journals about the bugs crawling on the window, and sneaking chapter books about the Galapagos into her textbook. We're now discovering that she can't spell and the teacher is worried about a possible disability." Merry's mom had valid reasons to be concerned, but I knew that Merry's story would continue to unfold in the future weeks, months, and years.

Merry's mom is a teacher in the same district where Merry goes to school. She has her Ph.D. in Educational Leadership. Her identity is also unfolding as her daughter makes her way through elementary school. Merry's mom is also gifted. She attended a school district close to the one in which she and Merry currently reside. Mom shared that she was identified as gifted in third grade but had to wait until sixth grade for access to the only formal services available. In junior high, she finally transferred to a school that allowed her walk to the high school for classes. She took courses for dual credit during her last few years of high school. She was considered a junior in college by the time she graduated from high school.

Merry's mom said that she had always wanted to be a zoologist. Selfishly, I am glad she did not take that path, because I would most likely not know her and daughter Merry. What you might discover in the stories that follow, is that Merry and her mom - although facing drastically different challenges - have more in common that what appears on the surface.

The global pandemic in 2020 presented new opportunities for Merry. This next section will provide a summary of the difficult decisions that were made to meet Merry's educational needs, and the many considerations in whether to send Merry back to school in the fall in a hybrid learning environment or pursue home schooling with a mom who best recognizes her child's needs.

•••

In February of 2020, before schools started to close due to the pandemic, Mom shared, "Merry was the only student in our district to place in the county-wide essay contest for grades 3-5. She has the highest STAR Reading score in the building. She holds the school record for highest 3rd grade state test score. She also has an "A" in every class EXCEPT reading/language arts."

When Merry was asked about this, she was clear and matter-of-fact, "It's boring and the teacher is mean."

Mom also shared, "Merry and a high school student adopted rabbits that had previously been paired and living in a barn. She read four huge books and watched multiple online videos on rabbit behavior. A week later, Merry's rabbit was roaming free in our house and fully litter trained. The other rabbit is still wild."

In working with her high school friend, Merry cautioned, "You can't hold him like he's a baby. He's a prey animal. Being on his back usually means he's about to die. If his cute little ears are up, he's scared." Mom commented, "Sometimes, I wish she was good at something that school gives trophies for, but animal behavior it is."

In February of 2020, Mom was thinking about the 2020-2021 school year, unaware of the impending pandemic. Mom shared, "I would love to 'unschool' her. Merry is a dancer who mastered a back handspring, split leap, and triple pirouette this year. But, she was so behind in PE, I had to have a conference with her teacher. She dances 13 hours a week and excels in her extracurricular, but she is only graded on running, throwing, and catching."

One day, Merry was being made fun of in gym while playing tug-of-war and reacted to the bully by saying, "I want to punch him in the face." The gym teacher advised against that reaction, saying, "Merry, there are cameras in here. You'll get a three day suspension if you do."

Merry thought for just a minute and delivered her argument, "I don't actually want to be here. That would be like a vacation."

Challenges continued in the beginning days of March. Merry's assignment in reading was to submit a word for Charlotte's web. Marry was excited because she loved animals and could envision herself talking with Wilbur the pig. She used a thesaurus, and selected the word 'prodigious', but her teacher could not accept it. The assignment was to cut the word out of a printed text, but Merry couldn't find that word in a newspaper or magazine. She refused to cut into a book, and Merry's mom agreed, so Merry had to find a new word.

Also in the beginning of March was the school's talent show. Merry, who you remember was behind in PE, choreographed and performed a complicated dance piece within three weeks. Her dance teacher was so impressed that she told Merry she could help her choreograph her own solo for the dance recital next year.

After this series of experiences, Mom reflected, "I just had an idea. Specials are already broken into three sections per grade level by home room. What if instead we broke them up by interests? We could have PE for the serious athletes, PE for the kids who just want to play dodgeball, and PE for the girls who spend all of recess dancing and flipping upside down. We could do the same with music: music for the kids who have a fit when they go to music, music for the kids who seriously want to read and play music, and music for the singers. Then the kids could decide if being in the tumbling/dance PE or the singing only music was more important to them."

In my honest opinion, Mom needs to be a principal. In her role as a teacher, she suggested some modifications to her teaching team when the pandemic hit hard. She suggested, "Let's take the kids outside last period instead of having science. It's 70 and sunny." Her colleagues responded, "Should we check with the administration?" Mom pointed out, "They're about to close the schools and modify the kids' learning experiences for the rest of the year. Let's give them a break. They need it."

As the pandemic shut life down for the spring and the rest of the school year, Merry's mom made some decisions for Merry's well-being as well as her own. Merry's mom stopped using her regular Facebook account and pared down her contacts to a newly created account that included only the people she needed and wanted to keep in her life.

Merry's mom quickly found that she enjoyed preparing online lessons and videos. She would take a selfie with the family's guinea pig and attach a link to a video that demonstrated how to draw a guinea pig. Her class went wild while learning about guinea pigs and how to draw them.

Merry was flourishing with learning at home. She began to discover new opportunities to challenge herself. For example, the family pup was a rescue and had brain damage. The dog would take off running in a random direction and wouldn't come back. Merry was very concerned, so she made a belt leash so that she can could play with him outside and have her hands free. This was just one of the many creative solutions Merry had the time and latitude to develop.

On the 9th day of homeschooling, Merry became tired of running upstairs to the linen closet to get paper towels and toilet paper. All of a sudden, there was a pulley system hanging from the family's 2nd story landing.

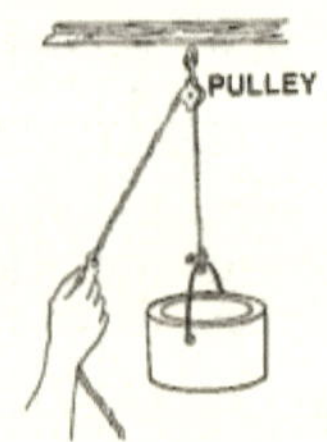

Mom found that she was doing a lot more unschooling than homeschooling. Merry would complete her daily work packet in about 30 minutes, or an hour if she had an essay to write. She chose to do her work outside under a tree and commented it was a good thing she didn't have to turn it in right away because it would smell like dirt. Mom pointed out that every aspiring teacher studies Gardener's Theory of Multiple Intelligences, yet we put students inside a cement building, forbid them from opening the windows, and count every minute to allow 20 minutes of recess on a blacktop lot. For kids whose strongest and most obvious intelligence is naturalistic, that seems to be a death sentence for potential and creativity.

Merry always had a point or an opinion. Most of her favorite books were in her mom's classroom and she just brought them home a few at a time. But, she wanted a new supply. Merry's mom tried to get her to go digital, but Merry felt like digital copies didn't "accurately capture the illustrations". In fact, Mom was surprised Merry was even asking for picture books. Mom observed that, without the stretch from Accelerated Reader, Merry could select picture books and read below her level. Mom pointed out that, when she was in second grade, she still liked picture books, too.

One day, Merry's mom emailed me: *"Do you think it is alright to let Merry take online classes designed for middle school, such as animal science? She's eight and, at least by age, a second grader."*

I asked: *"What does Merry think?"*

I was not surprised by her answer: *"She really wants to do that!"*

So, Mom registered her and Merry wrote her introduction on the discussion board, alongside the middle school students:

Camden: I'm Camden. I love animals, which is why I joined this class. One of my main career options is to be a veterinarian. I have spent a little time studying cat and dog anatomy and physiology. I am excited for this class!

Austin: I am Austin. I also love animals which is why I joined this class. I have always wanted to be someone who studies animals. I am especially into marine biology. I cannot wait for the class.

Charlotte: Hi, my name is Charlotte. I have loved animals my whole life and that is why I wanted to join this class. When I am a grown up, I want to be a veterinarian.

Mila: Hi, my name is Mila. I love animals, especially my cat Timmy.

Elizabeth: Hi, my name is Elizabeth. I love animals, including my dog and cat.

Eva: Hi, my name is Eva. I love animals. That is why I joined this class. I am so excited.

Merry: Hi! I'm Merry. I have loved animals ever since I was young, and I am always eager to learn more. My favorite animal is the pangolin. I am really happy to join this class.

After Mom saw all of the introductions, she commented, "Merry has apparently loved animals since she was young. How old does she think she is now?" I responded, "Well, I can guess how old she is cognitively."

Mom later shared one of the most exciting lessons taught by the presenting professor in the middle school online animal science class, "Marine Folklore and Apex Predators".

Merry explained:

> The professor started the Ocean's Daughter Conservation Alliance. It is like a 'save marine life' club. She is a doctor, like my mom, only this doctor is an expert in biochemistry, which means she knows all about the insides of living things. Biochemistry was just one word we learned today. Another word is 'apex' and 'predator'. Do you know what those words mean? Well, I can tell you. A predator is something that preys upon something else. Notice that isn't like we do in church. Prey means something that is hunted by, guess who? A predator. We also learned about the word 'apex'. Apex alone is the highest but if it is used with predator, that means that animal is the one who preys on other animals but there is no animal that preys on the apex. The professor also shared folklore of apex predators. Folklore is not like a fairytale but it is a story that people really believe even though they can't prove it really happened. Isn't that exciting that I learned that today?

Mom complimented the professor and her ability to address the asynchronous development; Merry is totally capable of learning the middle school content but also makes certain her stuffed giraffe is at her side when online.

I was really excited to hear how Merry's online learning was going. Then, Merry's public school reading teacher checked in on an assignment she had given Merry to complete at home. The conversation went like this:

Merry: I already did all these reading worksheets earlier this year for homework.

Teacher: I wanted to give you something I knew you could do on your own.

Merry: Do I have to do it again?

Teacher: Yes.

Merry: Can I turn in the old one?

Teacher: No. It's already graded.

Merry: Yeah. I know. I got a 100.

Clearly, the teacher does not know Merry, but her mom does. So, Mom made a deal with Merry. If she completed her school-issued worksheets for the week on Monday, Mom wouldn't mention them for the other 6 days.

K-W-L Chart

Topic: ______

What I Know	What I Want to Know	What I Learned

There were several other assignments that bothered Merry, one of which was KWL charts. These charts are divided into three sections for analysis, including what the student knows about a particular subject, what they want to know, and what they learned. In analyzing their unit on the French and Indian war, she replied with:

K: *I don't know anything about the French and Indian War.*
W: *I don't know enough about it to tell you what I want to learn.*
L: *Even if I knew what I wanted to learn, you aren't going to change what you are teaching about it.*

Merry's mom suggested some edits before submitting...

By the end of April, Merry commented that she LOVED her homeschool schedule. At school, she got one period of science, one period of social studies, two periods of reading, two periods of math, and one period of specials (music) 45 minutes a week. There was no art. With homeschool, she was taking a weekly art class, daily piano lessons, world music once a week, and science as often as she likes. Mom recorded the Jane Goodall special and watched it with Merry, complete with popcorn. They watched the meteor shower because they had a great view out in the country without light pollution. Merry also mentioned enjoying that she didn't have to deal with the kids at her school who would rather be in PE during music.

This was when Merry's mom really became confident in her thoughts to continue homeschool in the fall. Mom shared with me, "It's almost certain Merry will not being going to school full time next year."

Merry's mom stumbled into several challenges with this decision. Remember that Merry's mom teaches in the same district where Merry goes to school. So, she would not have childcare for Merry if she did not return. However, she also did not see the point in teaching her at home using someone else's materials, especially when those materials were likely ones that Merry has already mastered.

Another challenge presented itself with the cancellation of all the summer camps Merry had wanted to attend. Merry's extracurricular activities would be continued during the summer, but she had so many special interests that those camps were intended to address. Merry was still thriving on the flexibility provided with homeschooling. So, Merry's mom continued to go through her checklist of decision making points. The bottom line was that the public school was not a good fit for her. There was no flexible seating and the assignments were mostly worksheet based.

Meanwhile, school officials were considering a disability diagnosis for Merry. While some teachers were reasonably good at accommodating a difference in learning, some refused to adapt. A 504 plan would help, but getting that accomplished in a pandemic was even less likely than before. Merry's mom scratched the surface in researching ADHD, but Merry's history of motor delays and difficulty with printing and coloring, it was increasingly possible that may have dyspraxia.

With Mom being an educator, she recognized the signs that were there. She knew that Merry didn't really need a dyspraxia diagnosis, but the school was too rigid for Merry's learning needs. There were no breaks, and sometimes Merry wasn't even allowed to use the bathroom. She had to sit in a traditional desk without fidgeting. Additionally, Merry needed a quiet testing environment, but she didn't have an IEP indicating individual testing. She also needed extended time in writing due to weak motor skills. She was failing PE. Even if Universal Design for Learning were used, Merry would find greater success. Within the dinosaur of our educational system, she needed a diagnosis in order to have her needs met in a traditional classroom.

Because of her mom, Merry continues to thrive at home. She even took a class to learn how to paint a bunny, and then taught her mom how to paint one. Merry's mom has subscriptions for geography and science magazines, which Merry enjoys. In the summer, Merry reads and takes comprehension quizzes, and does math from Engage New York. These resoucres are free. She also uses her tablet for fact fluency and individualized math (free with Splash Math).

With the pandemic, Mom decided to incorporate history lessons using the Who Was books. Merry's mom remembers this was also how her parents "did" summer. Her dad would always remind her, "You never stop learning." Mom was just coming to the realization that not everyone, even among the "good" parents, does what her parents did for her and what she is now doing for Merry.

Merry's mom did her best to facilitate learning for all students. During the pandemic, she would drive to pick up a work packet from a student who had to move in with his grandmother where there was no internet service. It was pretty far from the school, but it is just what she does as an educator. Merry would ride along, observing the world as it went by. Once, Merry noted a spider and her possible condition. "Awww! Look, mom! I think she has babies!" This was shortly after a morning sighting of baby foxes on their land. Merry was thriving! And because of Mom's care of her students, they were also moving forward.

Merry's problem solving was continuing to flow, even with something as simple as bubble wands. When they ran out of bubble wands, Merry made an okay sign with her fingers and blew – and it worked.

Merry had many questions for her mom about the schools reopening. Merry's mom reviewed with her the CDC guidelines and the Ohio School Reopening Survey. Merry knew what she had to do; she wrote Governor Mike DeWine. Merry was very reasonable; she stated that she was concerned that not all students would have masks, and thought it would make perfect sense to start a sewing club to teach students how to make them for other kids at school. She also shared her concern about students who didn't have their own supplies and had to borrow from the teacher. Because she is an elementary student, she advocated playground reopening, and she proposed equipping all students with sanitizers as they enter the building. She also boldly pointed out that schools have more kids than adults, but adults are making all the decisions.

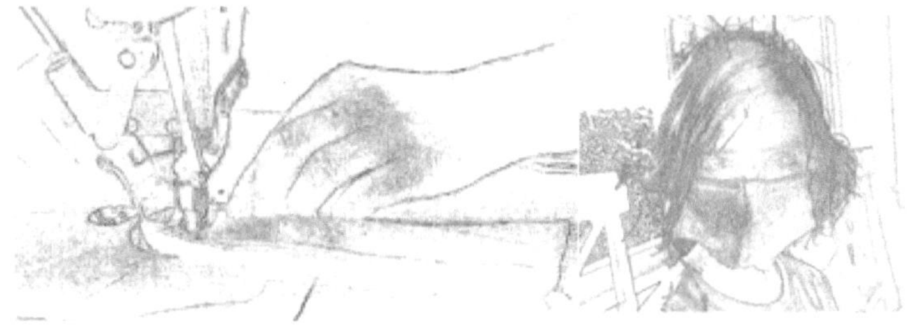

Summer camp was ultimately revived, but in a virtual format. Merry and the other virtual campers had to write a report to summarize what they learned. Merry titled her report, "The Ocean Food Chain from Plankton to Orca." In it, she misspelled several words: known, plankton, microscopic, organisms, penguin, leopard, and carnivores. When asked to spell each word orally, she spelled them correctly. She clearly knew how to spell each word. Merry's mom rationalized that she could give them to her like an oral spelling test instead, because when Merry writes something, the spelling turns off.

Merry does okay on her spelling tests if you twist her arm, but her writing is atrocious. She passed with mediocre marks in second grade. Mom is still chuckling that she won the third grade writing contest and has a plaque to prove it. Merry wrote about why Neville Longbottom was the best dog. It was important to her. In reflecting on math computation, Merry has figured out that she needs to be able to pace herself in order to think about math properly.

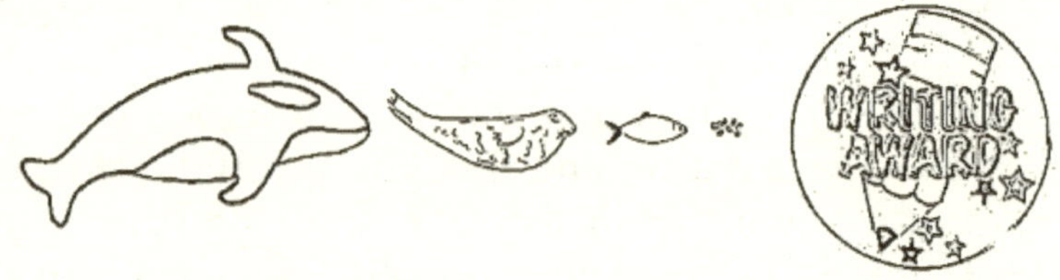

A new principal began working at Merry's school. With consideration of the many decisions that needed to be made, this new administrator answered all of Mom's questions regarding what she could provide her own first graders online in the new year. The answer sounded somewhat simple, "You can teach whatever you want as long as you 'cover the standards.'"

Merry's mom thought about that answer with math in mind, as there was no existing math curriculum to use. Then, a first grade math teacher mentioned downloading a curriculum from *Teachers Pay Teachers* for $800. Particularly at a time when virtual learning was proving difficult for some educators, this website provided a marketplace for teachers to purchase previously constructed lesson plans with learning materials.

In addition to online learning presenting difficulties for some of her students, Merry's mom felt that state testing was ruining the education of her students. Merry, for example, knew that the Eiffel Tower was in Paris, but not that Paris was in France or that France was a country. She did not know how many stripes or stars to include on the U.S. flag, or what the 13 original colonies were. Merry's mom expressed frustration, "Social studies isn't tested by the state until junior high, so nobody cares why my second grader has never heard of the Underground Railroad or why my rising 4th grader doesn't know about the colonies.

Merry's mom soon found out that her daughter's social studies and science time slots on the schedule was really designated as time for test prep. Upon learning what really motivated Merry in social studies, Mom signed her up for American History with American Girl Dolls on Outschool.

•••

Merry's mom is not alone in deciding to homeschool; many parents make the same decision. In choosing to homeschool, however, Merry gained the flexibility to take classes outside of her normal curriculum. Merry's Principal was flexible in allowing her to take outside classes, but it was an ongoing process to manage. Sometimes, she had to be late to one of her regular classes in order to make time for outside learning.

As businesses learned to adapt in the pandemic, Merry finally went back to her dance studio and got to see some of her friends! She became overwhelmed and started crying. She was excited to learn dances from Thailand, forms of expression she learned is even more important to the country than art. She was anxious to tell her mom what she had learned, "Did you know that they call it Thai dance, not Thailand dance? It is a tradition just like in other places in Asia. Thai dance is a high art if it is like classical dance and a low art if it is like folk dancing. I have learned both of those in dance class. And guess what? Our dance teacher asked if I could bring a stuffed elephant to our next class."

Merry's mom said, "Oh good! Look! We have one!"

Merry was kind about it, but had to correct her mom, "Mom! That's an African elephant. I need an Asian elephant. They have smaller ears."

Friendships were often difficult for Merry. Merry's mom shared, "I'm concerned that Merry only has one friend. Most of the kids like her, but there are only two girls in the "high" group. Her mom just pulled her to homeschool, and I am sort of panicking."

Sometimes, relatives can also be friends. Merry's mom has friends who own a petting zoo, so Merry and two of her cousins were given a private petting zoo tour. "This is COVID, their baby skunk. It slept on Merry's shoulder."

The Restart and Return plan in Merry's school district said that, if parents decide to continue with remote learning, their child has to come to school one day a week for classroom tests. Why, you might ask? Because of the standard grading system. Merry's mom reacted negatively to this news, "My students are 7...am I a teacher or a test proctor?!" Merry's mom rightfully questioned the district's perception of her role as an educator.

Meanwhile, local schools want students to bring lunches with only disposable sacks and containers. Merry's mom observed, "My little tree hugger is going nuts. I found paper instead of plastic, but they need to purchase a recycling bin before she has a cow."

The county in which they live is struggling in other ways. Merry's mom wrote, "Our county is in the red with COVID-19. Now, they say if we go fully remote, I will have to report to the school building and find daycare for Merry, which isn't any safer than her being at school. I'm hoping that changes."

Later, Merry's mom excitedly wrote to me, "After much prayer, a wonderful option fell from heaven and straight into my lap! Merry's dance teacher works daycare during the day. She has decided to keep a small group of girls, no more than 10, at the studio. They will each do their own virtual schooling and she will supervise. It will mostly be the girls on her dance team, which greatly reduces Merry's exposure. This way, she can keep up her extra classes like French and piano. Plus, the dance teacher has them scheduled to work and then take breaks for things like yoga. Even better, she'll go from class right to dance, so I don't have to rush to get her there."

Merry's mom shared another anecdote, prefacing the story by saying, "Everybody needs at least one friend who is a bigger nerd than they are, just for very specific emergencies." Decades ago, Merry's mom had read all but the last book in the *Unicorn Chronicles* series written by Bruce Coville. Merry had recently taken an interest in the series herself. Merry's mom had been waiting since 1996 to learn what happened in the final book, and with Merry now experiencing a similar itch, she searched for a copy. Unfortunately the cheapest one she could find was at Goodwill for $70. Her friend Shawn gave some solace, "I know a guy in Michigan...". Sure enough, he located a damaged copy for $30 with shipping. Merry and her mom shared in finally getting their hands on what happened next.

In conversations with other parents, Merry's mom learned that they had created their own home classrooms using Dollar Tree supplies. Their children even had their own desks! They could sit and do their work at their desks, distraction free. Meanwhile, Merry was on the floor surrounded by American Girl dolls and a handful of Brazilian rainforest animals. Merry's mom would put a math worksheet on a clipboard and say to her daughter, "Okay, Dr. Wilson! Time to fill out your paperwork!" Merry would then proceed to do her homework on the floor while feeding pretend sweet potatoes to an imaginary sloth.

The challenges continued for Merry's mom in her role as a teacher to 7 year olds. "Sometimes, I think I am doing this wrong," she said. "I have 3 groups of students: in-person, virtual, and remote with papers and flash drives. The reading series isn't in. The flash drives aren't in. The laptops aren't in. They have already taken our classroom laptops. I feel as if I am walking into The Hunger Games on Monday."

Meanwhile, Merry hadn't done any formal reading exercises since March. The only writing she completed was reports for her animal class. Yet, miraculously, her standardized test scores went up 2.5 years. Merry's mom wondered, "Is just leaving her alone an option?"

I told her I was in support of that, especially when it came to reading. Merry needed some direct instruction in math, particularly because they didn't have a remote math teacher this year. Her regular math teacher assigned her work, but had to teach in-person students all day, so Merry instead began working with a tutor. I supported Merry's mom in allowing her daughter to read at whatever level she felt most compelled to at the time. Merry might be on 11th grade literature, but as she approaches 9th grade, she would need some Judy Blume!

Merry made it clear that she loves homeschool, so Merry's mom is considering pulling her out if remote learning options disappear. Merry's STAR scores were the highest they had ever been, both score and percentile rank, after being home.

Although the school psychologist expressed concerns about Merry's social development, Mom reinforced that she dances 4 hours every night with other children her age. Merry had been in school for six years and it hadn't helped her social skills as much as dancing and taking middle school science online.

Merry's mom pondered the best curricular supports for homeschool math. "Math U See or good old Saxon? I have been so overwhelmed that I didn't even think about it. They have me teaching kids in-person five days a week, a virtual group, plus recording videos for flash drives for kids that don't have Internet. My brain is cooked. I'm just tired. Same pay. The union is not very happy."

In a final snapshot review of Merry's progress:

Merry turned 3 part way through the school year, but the preschool she attended had rolling enrollment. As long as a spot was open, they could begin when they turned 3, so she started in January. At that point, she was writing her name and reading.

Preschool - She was still 3 when she started her second year of preschool. They performed her gifted evaluation at the end of the year when she was 4, and agreed to Early Entrance Kindergarten..

At age 4, Merry went to Kindergarten.

At age 5, Merry was in first grade. This was the start of standardized testing. It was suggested that she could be accelerated to second grade, but board policy prohibits more than one grade acceleration.

At age 6, Merry was in second grade.

At age 7, she was in third grade. Her standardized test scores were still climbing and she was several years advanced in reading. The school contacted Merry's mom to see if they could place her in 4th grade for reading only. She declined. It was still about 5 years below her current reading level, and mom felt that it would make her stand out even more. She was worried about the social ramifications. She read at home, so there was not going to be a gap.

At age 8, Merry was a fourth grader. After a very successful journey into remote learning, the decision has been made to homeschool.

Merry's entire homeschool curriculum now takes 2 hours, and she loves it. Merry's parents have agreed to leave her enrolled in remote learning. Should that option no longer be available, they will homeschool. I am certain there will be more stories of Merry and her mom, so I am anticipating Passing on the Left – Part Two!

Think About: The Sensational Sensibilities, Myths, and Identity Journey details found in The Story of Merry - and also Merry's mom.

Passing on the Left	Sensational Sensibilities	Myth or Reality	Identity Journey
	Awarenesses – Sensual Energetic – Psychomotor Feelings – Emotions Imagining – Imagination Thinking – Intellectual	Myths that are believed by the gifted individual or others in the family, friends,and/or larger community	Frames Recognition - Validation Confirmation - Affirmation Connections - Affiliation Preferences – Affinity Compass Contributors You Your Immediate Family Your Ancestry Your Origins Career Explorations Living Spaces Educational Routes Relationships Experiences Legislations Attributes Phases
Merry			
Merry's mom			

The Story of Gavin

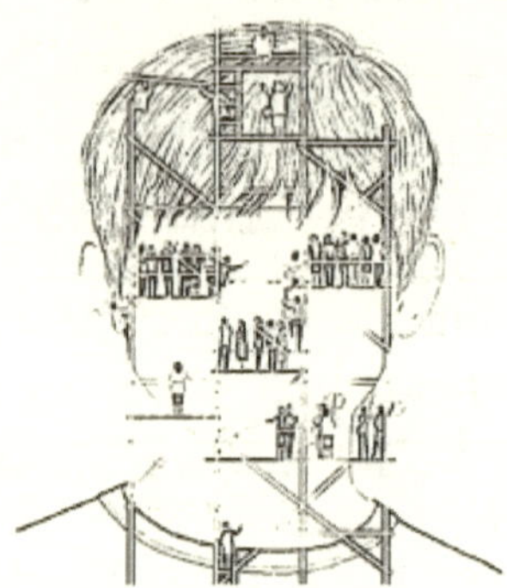

This is Gavin, a third grade student who was new to the gifted self-contained class in the school where I was principal.

Gavin was one of the first Asperger's Syndrome placements in our gifted program. He knew he was very capable in mathematics, and so did our gifted identification and placement committee.

In grades K-2, he was placed in heterogeneously grouped classrooms. When math was not presented at the advanced level he understood, he was prone to outbursts, and when his desk was moved, it presented difficulties in the classroom. Gavin's behavioral issues were the only thing defining him.

In 3rd grade, Gavin was officially identified as gifted and joined a group of other identified students in a self-contained gifted classroom taught by a teacher with a gifted endorsement. Unfortunately, however, none of my teachers had received training in how to meet the needs of children on the spectrum. As a principal, I had also not received this training. In fact, Gavin's mother attended a training and then came back to our staff to share what she had learned. Yes, we were trained by one of our parents. She was marvelous and a true partnership was developed.

Gavin needed sensory processing disorder therapy, which often involves a sensory immersion technique known as brushing. This would require a student's learning to be disrupted - sometimes multiple times a day - for regular immersion. It also had the potential to draw unwanted attention from other students. Instead, we had him use a plastic crate to collect books to return to the media center every day. The weight of the books in the crate resulted in the same decreased levels of defensiveness and anxiety as brushing therapy.

It was interesting that a child with Asperger's Syndrome would not automatically receive special education services or be given an Individualized Education Plan (IEP) once the diagnosis was made. The diagnosis was instead considered as part of the process for determining eligibility for special education services. When a student has a diagnosis of Asperger's Syndrome, developing a 504 Plan would give that student access to the accommodations needed to be successful. A 504 Plan was deemed less restrictive than an IEP and was typically implemented in the regular education classroom. We implemented a 504 for Gavin in his 3rd grade gifted self-contained classroom.

At the time, there were no formal gifted services at the secondary level for Gavin, but we did have something in place that helped tremendously. In addition to the 504, which followed him to grade 6, Academic Enrichment Advisors were in each of our K-12 schools. They met with the gifted coordinator once a month to plan activities that tied the program across the district. Identification and service processes flowed through the network of educators across our large district, and helped in gathering information for state reports. Those duties were not the most important aspect of their positions.

The advisor for Gavin's middle school made certain that she

met with his teachers and provided the same suggestions that had worked for us at the elementary level. At the middle school level, he continued in advanced math classes, but also added other areas. As Gavin grew into his identity, he discovered a love of leadership and writing/publishing. He became a co-editor of PawPrints, the middle school's literary magazine publication. Under his leadership in eighth grade, and with the other student co-director, Chelsea, PawPrints was the only middle school literary magazine in the nation to receive the highest award from the National Council of Teachers of English. The news coverage of this honor included quotes from his principal and the Academic Enrichment Advisor.

Middle School Wins Award for Literary Magazine

The best quote in the article was from Gavin and his co-editor in a letter written to their Literary Magazine Pawprints readers:

> *Middle school is a time of change and uncertainty. It is also a time for exploration. While students search for a sense of belonging and identity, they embark on many journeys. They experience struggles along the way, but when they emerge they do so with new visions. These journeys, struggles, and visions are not those of our parents or our teachers or the teenagers shown in the media. They are the box checked 'other'. Our own unique perspectives … and our writing and artwork are expressions from the heart.*

Once in high school, Gavin was able to accelerate his learning through advanced mathematics classes and College Credit Plus. His path after high school graduation looked like this:

- Studied Mathematics at University of Chicago Class of 2011
- Studied Mathematics at University of Michigan Ph.D. Class of 2017
- Graduate Student Instructor at University of Michigan
- Maths postdoc at University of Bristol Bristol, United Kingdom - present

Gavin has come a long way from his elementary school days and having to be the best in every math competition. Here he is smiling about his third place ranking next to a friend who took first place. The award was at the Young Mathematicians Conference and for the Outstanding Presentation Competition.

When one has the ability to compute math problems in their head, they often cannot explain their thinking. When teaching others, it is important to consider your process and have your students do the same. Gavin worked hard to be a treasured graduate student instructor.

Hard work and planning pays off when you are able to teach students who love math almost as much as you do.

Bristol England Post Doc

Gavin is now a "Post Doc" in Bristol, England, meaning that he is a scholar who professionally conducts research after having completed his doctoral studies. The ultimate goal for Gavin is to design and manage additional research, training, and/or teaching so he can realize a career in academia. He has researched and published solo in the SIAM Journal on Applied Algebra and Geometry and as a team of researchers in Journal of Number Theory, Journal of Theoretical Probability, Advances in Cryptology, and Fibonacci Quarterly.

I am staying in close contact to see what is next for this amazing person!

Think About: The Sensational Sensibilities, Myths, and Identity Journey details found in The Story of Gavin

Passing on the Left	Sensational Sensibilities	Myth or Reality	Identity Journey
	Awarenesses – Sensual Energetic – Psychomotor Feelings – Emotions Imagining – Imagination Thinking – Intellectual	Myths that are believed by the gifted individual or others in the family, friends,and/or larger community	Frames Recognition - Validation Confirmation - Affirmation Connections - Affiliation Preferences – Affinity Compass Contributors You Your Immediate Family Your Ancestry Your Origins Career Explorations Living Spaces Educational Routes Relationships Experiences Legislations Attributes Phases
Gavin			

The Story of the Essexers:
The Martin W. Essex School for the Gifted™

From the beginning of its existence, The Martin W. Essex School for the Gifted™ has offered Ohio's gifted high school students a unique opportunity to consider their vision of the future. The school was founded in 1976 and named for Dr. Martin W. Essex, Ohio's superintendent of public instruction from 1966-1976. This one-week residential program, included in the Ohio legislative budget, supported by the Ohio Department of Education, and hosted at The Ohio State University, emphasized leadership and social responsibility for students of exceptional abilities. Students took courses across the disciplines during the day. At night, students talked and did not get much sleep, because they had often found a group of new friends who were similar in nature in some ways and very different in others.

"FRIENDSHIP IS BORN
AT THAT MOMENT
WHEN ONE PERSON
SAYS TO ANOTHER,
'WHAT! YOU TOO?
I THOUGHT I WAS
THE ONLY ONE.'"
C.S. LEWIS

Some Essexers (what Essex students are called) have had gifted services of some type in their school district, whether in a formal program or cluster grouping in the regular classroom. However, many do not exactly know what being gifted is all about – it has not been explained either by parents or teachers. Most have not met many others, all gathered together in one place, who think and feel like they do.

The Ohio Department of Education published and distributed an Essex yearbook every year from 1979 until 2010, creating a consistent awareness in the 614 school districts in Ohio.

Essex and Governor's Summer Institute Budget Cut

In 2009, the legislature decided to pull the funding for both Essex and the Governor's Summer Institutes. The last year for Essex at OSU was 2010. Essex needed to find a new home and Otterbein University applied to be that recipient. The Ohio Department of Education was no longer a supporter of the Essex School.

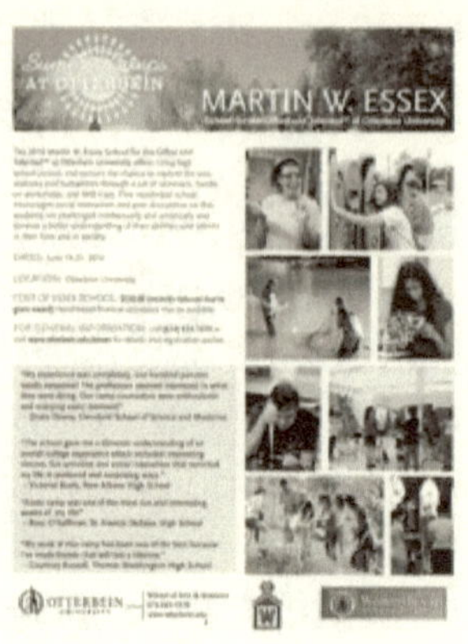

In 2011, the school officially moved to Otterbein University. Due to the lack of funding from the state of Ohio, new streams of financial support had to be found. Essex at Otterbein was made possible through tuition, as well as grants and scholarships from the Ohio Association for Gifted Children, Support for Talented Students, and the Martha Holden Jennings Foundation. It also benefitted from lunch and dinner donations provided by restaurants in the Otterbein home town of Westerville in order to reduce the costs of meals. An attempt was made to assure that any student who qualified for and desired to attend Essex at Otterbein could do so.

There were additional changes when the move was made to Otterbein. Applicants to Essex at OSU had to demonstrate superior cognitive ability to be considered. Since 1976 when the school was founded, other areas of giftedness have not only been recognized but also made part of the required identification of gifted in the state of Ohio. In addition, Essex at OSU was only for rising seniors in high school. The loss of funding for the Governor's Summer Institutes meant that fewer gifted rising juniors had options for summer programs. Therefore, applicants to Essex at Otterbein were rising juniors and seniors in high school and gifted in any of the areas recognized by the Gifted Operating Standards:

Cognitive Ability
Specific Academic Ability
Creative Thinking Ability
Visual/Performing Arts (Art, music, dance, drama)
Twice Exceptional

We therefore made an adjustment to the name of the school:

The Martin W. Essex School for the Gifted and Talented™ at Otterbein University

The biggest variance for Essex came in 2020, at the will of the global pandemic. A residential program was not going to be a possibility; we faced the decision of taking Essex virtual or canceling it altogether. We believed that an interruption in hosting Essex would cost us momentum and possibly the continuation of the school itself. Fortunately, a course shell for a high school College Credit Plus option was identified as a perfect fit for the week-long agenda. All students were registered for this course, a design of the Essex sessions was built around the course focus of leadership, and those who wished to take the course for college credit were able to pay that tuition. Students examined their own contributions as leaders and also experienced sessions including:

Sunday, June 14: **Welcome and Leadership Storytelling Evening Activity**

Monday, June 15: **Leadership and Identity Development with a Storytelling Evening Activity**

Tuesday, June 16: **Leadership and Your Head and Heart with a Storytelling Evening Activity**

Wednesday, June 17: **Leadership and the Voices within Us with a Storytelling Evening Activity**

Thursday, June 18: **Leadership and Mathematics with a Storytelling Evening Activity**

Friday, June 19: **Leadership and the Common Book Dreamland with Essex Graduation**

During the year of planning for the 2020 program, it was decided that Essex would once again have to find a new home. The pandemic made it necessary for Essex 2020 to be an online offering. Meanwhile, Otterbein was experiencing a reduction in student population and, therefore, a reduction and reassignment of professors. Ashland University eagerly became the recipient of the school with application and receipt of a High Impact Grant, so that the school can experience a smooth move for June 2021. It has already been decided that the school will once again have to be virtual. Already in place in the fall of 2020, is a steering committee comprised of gifted advocates and professionals with strengths they are willing to contribute to assure an offering that will meet and exceed prior schools.

As with the move to Otterbein, there are adjustments being made as Essex moves to its new home. Rising sophomores are being added to the list of those qualified to apply for the school. We are framing 2021 Essex as TRANSITIONING to a new home, moving from Otterbein University to Ashland University. The design of the school is also TRANSFORMING, taking the best from the past Essex Schools and past Governor's Summer Institutes. Each morning, a keynote will set the stage for leadership experiences through the lens of change: connected to identity development, leading through with the head and the heart, leadership in literature, leadership in mathematics, and leadership styles. The afternoon will be devoted to daily, in-depth small-group instruction in a topic of passion by an expert in the field. This mentorship will be carried throughout the afternoons of the 5 days of Essex.

One of the first Essex experiences focuses on identity

development, the myths and realities of giftedness, and overexcitabilities (Farrenkopf, 2020). Students discuss common myths that others, even themselves, had believed true. There is often an audible sigh of relief when we discuss the myth that gifted could and should be perfect. Reflecting individually on the five overexcitabilities, Essexers are asked to determine which characteristics are most like them. They then work in groups to generate a list of what they want their parents and teachers to know about the joys and frustrations of these intensities, and advice for providing support. An example of one list follows:

Awareness (Your Senses)
Joys: Music, Art, Debating
Frustrations: Unnecessary noise, smelly smells, lotion – AXE!
Advice: Let us talk – don't overuse perfume

Energetic (Psychomotor)
Joys: Lots of energy and love competitions
Frustrations: Can't sit still, overstimulated, never sleep
Advice: Give assignments that involve movement

Feelings (Emotional)
Joys: Easily communicate emotionally with others (sympathize /empathize)
Frustrations: Overreact, too strong emotions in certain situations, conveying emotions is difficult
Advice: Let us express our emotions

Thinking (Intellectual)
Joys: Fun facts, independent, high-quality ideas, good under pressure
Frustrations: Don't work well with others, don't like fixed pace, procrastinate
Advice: Let us do independent work

Imagination (Imaginational)
Joys: Creative abilities, lack of boredom, able to picture things, idealistic
Frustrations: Trouble focusing, procrastination, bounce from topic to topic
Advice: Engage us and allow to work in small groups, "switch it up", involve more creative thinking in class

Then there is the topic of identity development. The Gifted Identity Formation Model (Mahoney, 1999) is used as a lens for this part of the session, with an adjustment in the terms to facilitate the time we have been able to carve out for this (Farrenkopf, 2020).

Shaping and Influencing the Journey
Four Frames

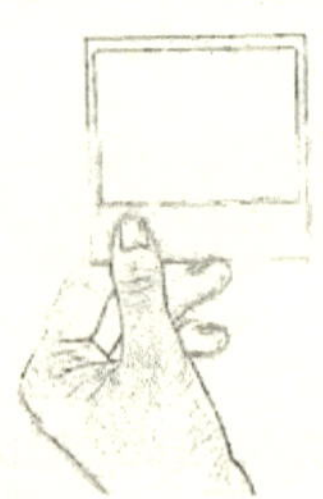

Recognition – The first step is the realization you are gifted.

Confirmation – Continued reinforcement that you are gifted.

Connections – Finding others who are like you.

Preferences – Finding the fit between your giftedness and your passion and purpose.

Compass Contributors to the Journey

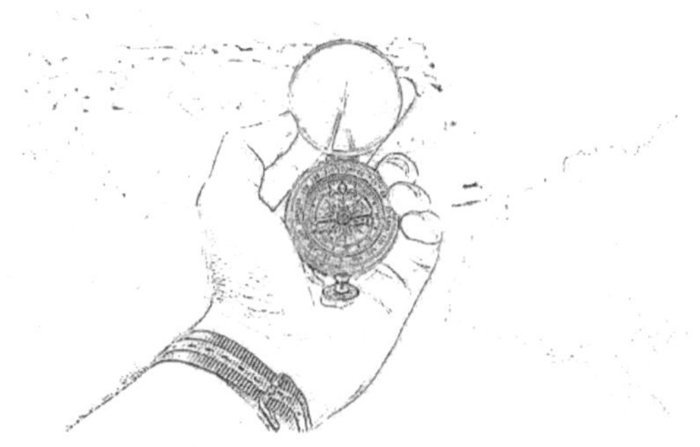

YOU (values and how you see yourself)

Your Immediate Family (parents, guardians, siblings)

Your Ancestry (past generations of your family)

Your Origins (heritage, gender, race, religion, and ethnicity)

Your Career Exposures (your own interests as well as family career history)

Your Living Spaces (where you work and play)

Your Educational Routes (where you learn both inside and outside of school)

Your Relationships (how you connect inside and outside of your family)

Your Experiences (preferences – including overexcitabilities)

Your Legislations (opportunities to support giftedness)

Your Attributes (how you are known – leader, lover of music, math mind, etc.)

Your Phases (stage of your learning – asynchronous development)

Evaluations are a very important part of the Essex School experience. Students complete daily reflections and also summarize their experience after the graduation. Here are some examples of what we heard from the Essexers in 2020:

What do you find to be the most challenging part of a gifted identity or a gifted identification?

I really did not see myself as "gifted." Expectations of others, intellectual isolation, general societal misunderstanding of what giftedness means, my own perceived failures and self-criticism created a fog for me.

Unreal expectations of others, intellectual and social isolation, limited peer groups, my own personal expectations are things to work through.

My biggest problem is with the general societal misunderstanding of what giftedness means. That really molded my personal expectations – and they can be unreal at times.

The complexity of my emotions is hard. On top of that, other people have expectations of me because I achieve, then I think I need to do better and put pressure on myself.

In one sentence, explain to a future Essex student what the "Essex Experience" is like.

An incredible opportunity to discover yourself and "unpack your story":)

Being immersed with people similar to yourself while exploring what makes you different has been life changing for me.

You will find yourself in others and make friends along the way.

The Essex Experience was truly amazing- it allowed me to better explore who I am and discover that my abilities are more complex than I thought.

I most definitely have deepened my sense of self.

Think About: The Sensational Sensibilities, Myths, and Identity Journey details found in The Story of the Essexers

Passing on the Left	Sensational Sensibilities	Myth or Reality	Identity Journey
	Awarenesses – Sensual Energetic – Psychomotor Feelings – Emotions Imagining – Imagination Thinking – Intellectual	Myths that are believed by the gifted individual or others in the family, friends,and/or larger community	<u>Frames</u> Recognition - Validation Confirmation - Affirmation Connections - Affiliation Preferences – Affinity <u>Compass Contributors</u> You Your Immediate Family Your Ancestry Your Origins Career Explorations Living Spaces Educational Routes Relationships Experiences Legislations Attributes Phases
The Essexers			

Story of Jonathan

Jonathan was born in the 1950s in a large urban city in the Midwest. His dad worked at the airbase nearby and was frequently involved in projects that took him out of the country. His mother was a stay-at-home housekeeper who had always wanted to go to college but was not permitted to do so by her parents, even though her baby sister was. Jonathan had one sibling, Jerry, who was three years older. His grandfather on his father's side lived with them.

Jonathan's neighbor was a real life Mr. Wilson from *Dennis the Menace;* his name was even Mr. Wilson. Jonathan liked to visit Mr. Wilson and enjoyed talking to him. Jonathan remembers starting school at age 4 - soon to be 5 - when he was standing in line to enter the classroom. He remembers the numbers and letters all looking very familiar. He remembers being one of two students assigned to get milk for the classroom snack. He remembers naps, and he remembers asking endless questions of his mom when he returned home from school each day.

In first grade, Jonathan was once again standing in line on the first day, waiting to enter his new classroom at Grover Elementary. He loved math early on, but was anxious to learn to read; his brother had told him to expect that in first grade. Jonathan vividly remembers being pulled out of the line on that first day to be placed in another class's line of students. When he located his class pictures years later he observed that, while attending his K-8 elementary school, the kids in his yearly photos were pretty much the same. He remembers being warned by kids on the playground of certain teachers, only to find out once he was assigned to their classrooms that he really liked them. They expected a lot and Jonathan was fine with that.

He was finding new opportunities as he advanced through the grades – beyond math and reading. One year, he even dabbled in drama as he was selected to be the Pied Piper.

Another year, he played Schroeder and a student he recalls he had a crush on played Lucy.

Reflecting on his classmates, Jonathan remembers students that he admired for their intelligence. There was Rod, who had an amazing ability in music. Even at a young age, he played the violin with feeling, and far before students began to even think about selecting a musical instrument or taking beginner lessons.

There was Earl, who could draw absolutely anything and had never had lessons outside of the art class scheduled once or twice each week. Earl's classmates would ask him to sketch anything from their caricature to a design for a new car after describing the features.

Even though Jonathan achieved high grades and was selected for two leading roles in his elementary school productions, he did not see himself as particularly smart. He remembers the times when he really had to work hard and, at the time, translated that into not being anywhere close to the top of his class.

A life-changing event for Americans occurred on November 22, 1963, when John F. Kennedy was assassinated. At the time, Jonathan's family had a black and white TV, and they watched the three-day sequence of events unfold as the president died, as his assassin was caught, and then as the assassin was murdered during live coverage of his transfer to prison.

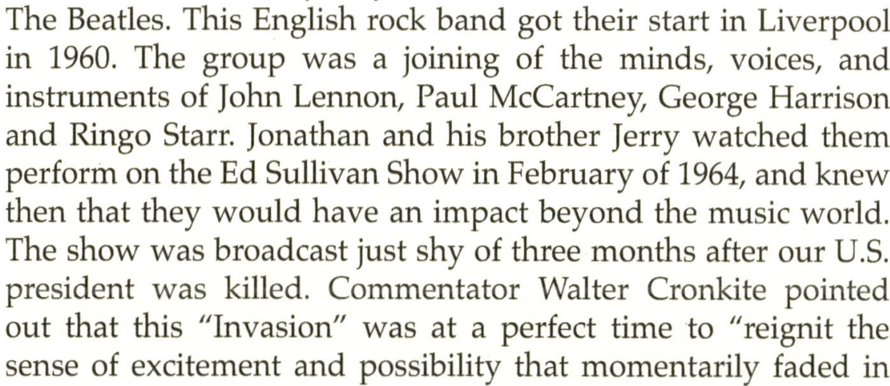

Another historical element from Jonathan's elementary days involved The Beatles. This English rock band got their start in Liverpool in 1960. The group was a joining of the minds, voices, and instruments of John Lennon, Paul McCartney, George Harrison and Ringo Starr. Jonathan and his brother Jerry watched them perform on the Ed Sullivan Show in February of 1964, and knew then that they would have an impact beyond the music world. The show was broadcast just shy of three months after our U.S. president was killed. Commentator Walter Cronkite pointed out that this "Invasion" was at a perfect time to "reignit the sense of excitement and possibility that momentarily faded in the wake of the president's assassination." The Beatles were a symbol of the soon-to-come revolutionary social changes in the 60s and 70s. Even their iconic hairstyle, mocked by adults, became a desired look for youth as a statement of rebellion. Both Jerry and Jonathan started working on their Beatle haircuts with the help of their cosmetology-trained mother.

Eighth grade flew by and it became time for Jonathan to attend First in Flight High School. Jerry was a senior when Jonathan started his freshman year. Jerry had shared with Jonathan that he hoped he would not get Mr. Rowland for math. Jonathan completely understood that wish and agreed. He had witnessed his brother struggling with the copious math assignments, crying in frustration when he could not complete all of the tasks, knowing that Mr. Rowland would record a bad homework grade and call him out in class.

Jonathan remembers well that first day of school when he stepped into his first period math class and the teacher introduced himself.

"Students, my name is Rowland, Mr. Rowland. You will work harder in my class this year than you ever have worked."

Jonathan had much to talk about with his brother that evening. He did indeed have Mr. Rowland for his freshman honors math class. As the year wore on, he noted that the freshman homework was often the same as that assigned to his brother in a non-honors, higher grade level math class. Jerry tried to console and help his brother, but knew that if he helped too much, Mr. Rowland would know.

Fortunately, Jonathan also had Mr. Camps for his honors English class. The reading list for this freshman course was very rigorous, but Jonathan loved every minute of it. He actually received comments on his homework and papers, specifically guiding him on how to think, rather than what to think. Many of Mr. Camps' comments were actually questions, and continued from the words on the paper into the discussions in class. Students had class discussions and learned that it was okay to not always agree, as long as you could explain your thinking.

Sports had always intrigued Jonathan, but he knew he wanted to avoid contact sports and overly competitive options. In 7th grade, he had asked his Mom to use her S&H stamps saved from grocery store purchases to buy a tennis racquet. He enjoyed talking to some older boys in the neighborhood and know that they also wanted to play tennis. Sometimes it was just on the street in front of his house and other times the boys hitched a ride to an open tennis court at a recreation center. This interest continued into high school, college, into Jonathan's adult life.

Another interest appeared when Miss Stanton, the fencing coach, made an announcement for all interested students to meet her in the gym after school. Jonathan was intrigued by fencing. It was like *The Three Musketeers*. It was part of the Olympics and used great vocabulary like Épée, Foil, Sabre, Body cord, Lamé, and Grip. It didn't hurt, either. It was known as a semi-contact sport.

A life lesson awaited Jonathan when he was not selected for an away match. In that moment, he decided to quit. He later decided to talk with Miss Stanton and ask if he could return. She said she would accept him back to the team, but did not want to see him quit again. He never did.

Another teacher marvel was Dr. Burkett. Although First in Flight High School had many great teachers, she was one of very few with a Ph.D. When a local high school closed, the principal Mr. Sherlock came to First in Flight and brought many of the teachers with him. Dr. Burkett was one of them. She, like Mr. Camps, provided meaningful feedback and guidance to influence a desire for knowledge in her students. She taught senior honors English and provided support for the writers of the graduation speeches for Baccalaureate and Commencement.

Jonathan, the boy who thought in

elementary school that he was far from the top of the class, graduated 7th in a class of 285. He was the president of the Honor Society at First in Flight High School, and was accepted into college with the intent to major in mathematics. After all, he had always been told he was good in mathematics.

Jonathan attributed his success in college to knowing how to study. He could not remember when or how he had learned the study techniques that worked for him, but it was clearly working for him.

It was working everywhere, except in math. College calculus arrived at imaginary numbers, and Jonathan looked around at the other students in his classroom. They clearly "got it" to a level that Jonathan was not experiencing. He changed his major to accounting.

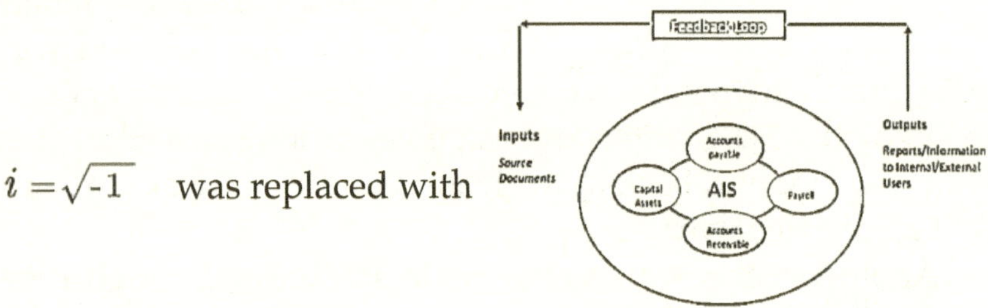

Fortunately, Jonathan roomed with a friend from high school and they both were serious about studying and doing their best. Studying for Jonathan meant finding a quiet place to concentrate. The dorm was not that place. Even the main library on campus was not the place; there was too much socializing going on there. He found a smaller department library that was open 24/7 and was not a popular place for students to do anything but study.

Jonathan's parents sacrificed a lot so they could send their two sons to college. When he received his quarterly college grades in the mail, the reports were always celebrated by his family.

At Christmas time, the transcript of his current progress went on the tree as an ornament. Jonathan recalls wanting to go to college and make his parents proud because they had sacrificed so much to make it possible for him. Even when the university closed early due to the 1970 war demonstrations and the Kent State tragedy, when asked to join the march, Jonathan declined. He simply said, "My parents are paying for me to go to college and I would not do that to them." He was certainly not for the Vietnam war, especially after drawing a draft number of 1. He would protest in different ways, like voting.

Jonathan proceeded through his college experience, enjoying the electives he took the most. He continued to do well in his accounting coursework and a professor even asked if he would consider tutoring students who were having difficulty. Jonathan was surprised by the question, responding that he didn't know if he would be the right person to tutor. The professor then shared a bit of insight that he was likely not supposed to communicate to anyone, "Well, I think you are more than capable. You are the number one graduate in the college of business."

Jonathan's senior year was a whirlwind as he accepted a recruiter's offer to join a prestigious accounting firm after graduation. Jonathan also married at the end of his senior year and moved to Columbus, Ohio to start a new chapter. Apartment hunting, training trips, and reconnecting with friends and family replaced going to classes, studying for tests, and walking uptown for a brew.

Within a year, his marriage crumbled and he was let go from the accounting firm. Reading this, one might feel sorry for Jonathan. Actually, it was for the best. At the time, marriage was just something expected at the end of college, and Jonathan was merely following in the path of his brother Jerry. The internal workings of the accounting firm did not match with Jonathan's need to develop work relationships that were authentic and involved more than drinking. When a partner told Jonathan that he did not like the way he walked, a needed change was in the air.

New friendships were formed outside of the business shell. Jonathan was discovering what he needed in friendship. He needed people who were deep, intelligent, and had a soul. He was searching for a new tribe, so to speak. He found success in banking and with a large industrial company as a senior accountant. His friendships grew through the people he found after his life seemed to crumble.

He started to read serious literature again, titles he had noticed in his honors English class as other suggested texts found in book reviews. He applied study skills learned early in life, only this time not to prepare for a test but to note unfamiliar words and keep a list of definitions. He also became reacquainted with his love of cycling and even became the business manager of a small bicycle shop after retiring from his senior accountant position at a local large industrial complex. He found a new love of work when combining a passion for cycling, a small and responsive business model, and new friends who had a myriad of characteristics and qualities about which Jonathan appreciated and resonated.

Then, another blip on the radar occurred. He reconnected with Patty, a high school friend whom he had not seen in 20 years. They discovered that they had been born in the same hospital 5 days apart. They already knew they had attended the same high school and college. Life had since taken them in different directions, but here they were connecting again. They had amazing conversations over lunch and on phone calls. She was an educator who had taught in public schools and was now a coordinator of gifted programs. They developed a true need to stay connected. Through their conversations, it was discovered that Jonathan did not have a clear picture of what his giftedness was and what it meant specifically for him.

The K-12 school district officials where Jonathan and Patty had attended K-12 school made an announcement that Grover and Benjamin Elementary School were going to be torn down and replaced with newer structures. It was time for a road trip.

Patty was able to call and schedule a time for a visit to these two brick and mortar reminders of their K-12 education. This "back to the future" tour of both schools provided a context for both Jonathan and Patty to share their memories.

Grover Elementary

Benjamin Elementary

One of the topics of discussion that day was the idea of requesting their school records. Patty was convinced that Jonathan would have high ability and achievement scores noted on his transcript. She was correct. When Jonathan's transcript arrived, she pointed to the 148 score and said, "See, I told you so. This is my business to know these things."

As Jonathan and Patty continued to develop their relationship, she would take him to presentations about gifted minds made from nationally known experts. One speaker shared the characteristics of gifted that could be challenging to understand. Patty looked over to say something to Jonathan, but he was already tearing up, whispering to her, "So, THAT is why I have always felt this way."

Jonathan popped the question to Patty and she accepted his proposal to marry. He had the idea of getting married on the beach and she researched how it would work to obtain a license for an out-of-state wedding. He knew they were a perfect couple, and explained, "I often have great ideas and you often implement them."

As of this writing in the fall of 2020, Jonathan and Patty have been happily married for almost 20 years. Normal times can be a challenge for many couples, and experiencing a pandemic can introduce incredible added pressures. But this couple is doing fine, problem solving through each day – each week – each month. Daily routines have continued with slight tweaks.

One routine is Lumosity, an online program consisting of games designed to improve memory, attention, flexibility, speed of processing, and problem solving. Jonathan is not certain he buys all of their claims, but he enjoys putting this on his daily schedule. The game allows players to track their scores compared to others in their age group range. Jonathan is currently at 98.8 (out of 100) and jokes that he is not making AYP (or average yearly progress) due to his age group. As soon as he "graduates" to a higher age group, he feels confident that he will be at the top of his class again. Jonathan believes that the knowledge he has will be that much more impressive when he's the youngest one in the room. In this, Jonathan understands the challenges of gifted students, demonstrating that when removed from age-specific assessments, students can better meet their individual challenges and academic needs.

Patty is a director of a summer experience for gifted high school juniors and seniors, and Jonathan quickly became the official photographer. Jonathan experimented with his digital camera and found that he had an eye for taking just the right shot at the right time. Because the camera is digital, it has become much easier for Jonathan to take a chance and push the button to capture what he sees, even if when seeing the result he decides to select delete. It is hard for Jonathan to accept compliments, but there is evidence of his talent, as his photos are shared and people comment they enjoy his work. He modestly accepts the accolades. He has continued to experiment with this technology, focusing on flora, animals and insects. A Christmas present of a macro lens has catapulted the quality of the photography to a new level.

Looking ahead to 2021, both Jonathan and Patty realize there is much yet to uncover or reveal about already discovered talents. Not all gifts are obvious or identified at one time; these areas of potential develop when you are with others who are of similar ability and who appreciate the possibility and desire to continue to grow. Those opportunities unfold throughout your lifetime. If you are interested in searching for them, there are people like you who are waiting to be discovered. Those windows of possibilities will appear in the most surprising places, and maybe even when you are on the bicycle path and passing on the left.

Photographs taken by Jonathan

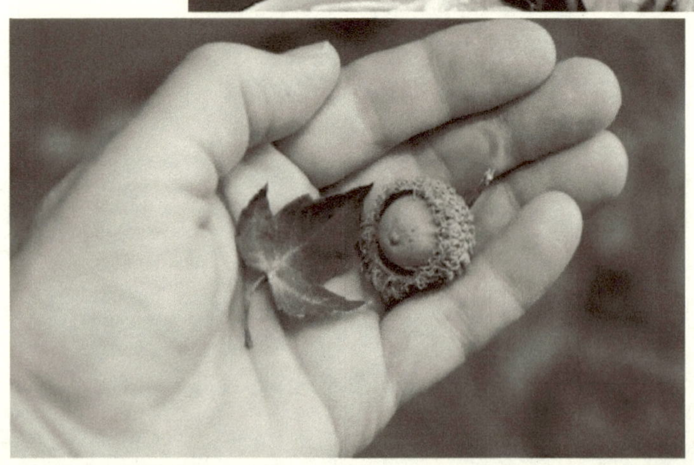

Think About:
The Sensational Sensibilities, Myths, and Identity Journey details found in The Story of Jonathan

Passing on the Left	Sensational Sensibilities	Myth or Reality	Identity Journey
	Awarenesses – Sensual Energetic – Psychomotor Feelings – Emotions Imagining – Imagination Thinking – Intellectual	Myths that are believed by the gifted individual or others in the family, friends,and/or larger community	<u>Frames</u> Recognition - Validation Confirmation - Affirmation Connections - Affiliation Preferences – Affinity <u>Compass Contributors</u> You Your Immediate Family Your Ancestry Your Origins Career Explorations Living Spaces Educational Routes Relationships Experiences Legislations Attributes Phases
Jonathan			

Appendix A – Summary Chart for Passing on the Left

Passing on the Left	Sensational Sensibilities	Myth or Reality	Identity Journey
Merry	Psychomotor Imaginational Intellectual	Myth: It is best not to accelerate more than one year.	From Validating to Affirming
Merry's mom	Imaginational Intellectual	Myth: Unless you have received training in gifted, you cannot tell if your daughter is gifted.	Affinity – returning to validation as she parents Merry
Gavin	Psychomotor Intellectual	Myth: Gifted students are good at everything and do not have any disabilities.	From Validation to affinity
Essexers	All of them represented	Myth: Gifted students are all the same.	Validating Affirming Affiliation with other Essexers
Jonathan	Intellectual Emotional	Myth: If you have to work hard, you are not really gifted.	Repeating all four identity stages as new information learned, new areas of interest identified, new relationships are formed

Arbour, T. (2019). The ohio trail vision. Columbus, OH: ODNR. Retrieved from: https://trails.ohiodnr.gov/wp-content/uploads/2019/05/Ohio_Trails_Vision-2019-SM.pdf

Farrenkopf, P. (2020). Identity Journey. Columbus, OH: Fishtail Publishing.

Farrenkopf, P. (2020). Myth or Reality. Columbus, OH: Fishtail Publishing.

Farrenkopf, P. (2020). Sensational Sensibilities. Columbus, OH: Fishtail Publishing.

Individuals with Disabilities Education Act (2020). IDEA news and updates. Retrieved from: https://sites.ed.gov/idea/idea-news-and-updates/#2020

League of American Wheelman (2019). Better bicycling traffic laws. Retrieved from: (https://bikeleague.org/content/traffic-laws

Magas, S. (2020). Bike lawyer. Retrieved from: https://www.ohiobikelawyer.com/bike-law-101/2010/01/ohios-bike-laws/

National Association for Gifted Children (2020). Resources for educators & parents during COVID-19. Retrieved from: https://www.nagc.org/resources-publications/resources/resources-educators-parents-during-covid-19

Ohio Department of Education (2018). Ohio operating standards for identifying and serving students who are gifted. Retrieved from: https://education.ohio.gov/getattachment/Topics/Other-Resources/Gifted-Education/Rules-Regulations-and-Policies-for-Gifted-Educatio/Ohio-Administrative-Code-3301-51-15.pdf.aspx?lang=en-US

Developing the Gifted Series

Order at www.fishtailpublishing.org

Volume 1

Sensational Sensibilities

Card deck available for purchase

Volume 2

Identity Journey

Card deck and activity sheet available for purchase

Volume 3

Myth or Reality?

Card deck available for purchase

Volume 4

Passing on the Left

Card deck and activity sheet available for purchase

www.ingramcontent.com/pod-product-compliance
Lightning Source LLC
LaVergne TN
LVHW051019080826
845145LV00009B/2707

9781733338066